MW01230754

In August 1979, rig took a trip through Canada with our travel trailer. Some of our main stops included Toronto, Quebec City, Montreal, Prince Edwards Island, and Moncton, New Brunswick. Our ultimate destination was Halifax, Nova Scotia. One of my favorite stops along the way was Peggy's Cove, Nova Scotia. I can still see the rocky shore, the towering lighthouse, and hear the ocean water as it washed against the rocks. Peggy's Cove felt like heaven on Earth to me.

The beautiful illustrations reflected on the cover of this book and throughout the interior were inspired by Peggy's Cove and created by my talented son, Austin.

Unimaginable Loss...
Godly Transformation
During the Age of COVID

A Grief Journey & Journal

*A woman's triumphant story of healing and acceptance
after losing three immediate family members.*

K. JOYNER

XULON ELITE

Xulon Press Elite
555 Winderley Pl, Suite 225
Maitland, FL 32751
407.339.4217
www.xulonpress.com

Paperback ISBN-13: 978-1-66288-328-6
Hard Cover ISBN-13: 978-1-66288-329-3
Ebook ISBN-13: 978-1-66288-337-8

Dedication

To God, who never left my side and gave me the peace that surpasses all understanding during a time when I needed Him the most. Who also brought individuals into my life at just the right time, and was patient enough to answer my questions or to help me discern the questions I may never know the answer to, at least while I am still here on Earth.

To my loved ones, Harry, Marian, and Troy Franklin, who taught me the importance of faith in God, storytelling, generosity, kindness, family, friends, music, and laughter. Your legacies live on through many of your friends who are now my friends; the stories they share of their time with you and the many people you impacted during your time on this earth. Your stories will continue through this book, which God inspired me to write, and through your grandchildren, Austin and Brooke, who will tell your stories to their children, their grandchildren, and on through the generations to come.

To my loving and devoted husband, Keith, who loved you, as well, and comforted me during the most horrific year I ever could have fathomed.

To my many aunts, uncles, and cousins who were by my side during that difficult year and remain by my side today.

We all miss you and love you more than the words expressed in this book could ever convey.

Foreword

IN THE WAKE of the global pandemic that shook the very foundation of our lives, many of us find ourselves grappling with unfathomable loss–the untimely departure of our loved ones from this world, victims of the devastating COVID-19 virus. The pain we bear is both personal and collective, as countless individuals across the globe have had to endure the heart-wrenching experience of bidding farewell to a cherished family member, friend, or acquaintance. Simply put, it has been a tough couple of years, and none of us came out of this pandemic unscathed.

Although the pandemic is over, the heartbreak is not. For those of us who experienced profound loss and grief, things have not gotten "back to normal." That is why it is essential that people of faith come together to encourage and support one another in the aftermath of this hopefully, once in a lifetime experience.

It is within this context that this book, *Unimaginable Loss... Godly Transformation* by Kelli Joyner emerges. This book is dedicated to acknowledging the profound impact and loss many of us have experienced during the pandemic–and the comfort, guidance, and hope for those who find themselves in the depths of sorrow.

Within the pages of this book, you will discover a woman's story of resilience, strength, and the indomitable human spirit. Kelli does a remarkable job describing her unforeseen journey and she allows us to walk with her, and her family, during these trying and devastating times. Through a myriad of perspectives and experiences, we are reminded that the human experience of grief is both universal and unique, and that in sharing our stories, we forge connections that can help mend the broken pieces of our hearts.

So, as you embark on this poignant voyage, I urge you to approach each page with an open heart and an open mind. Embrace the rawness and vulnerability of her story, for within their depths lie seeds of healing and transformation. While grief may seem an endless abyss, her story offers glimpses of light–a reminder that even amiss darkness, there is the potential for growth, meaning, and a renewed sense of purpose.

In the spirit of unity and compassion, let us come together, lifting one another up, and creating a world where grief is met with empathy and understanding. May this book serve as a testament to the resilience of the human spirit and a source of solace for all those who have experienced the profound loss of loved ones.

With heartfelt wishes for healing and hope,
LEE JENKINS, Senior Pastor
Eagles Nest Church, Roswell, GA

Preface

GROWING UP AND on into adulthood, I always felt I had a perfect life. I had wonderful, loving, Christian parents who served tirelessly as sport coaches, scout leaders, and supportive attendees during every activity my brother and I pursued. As an adult, I had a great career, a caring and devoted husband, two wonderful children, an extensive and close-knit extended family, and a host of great friends. Things always worked out for me. My daddy used to tell me, "You live a charmed life," and I always believed him. Life always worked out for me, and I felt God's favor with every pursuit.

All of that changed during the COVID-19 pandemic when I lost three immediate family members within five and a half months. My trust in the Lord to work everything out for me was shaken. One of the questions with which I have been wrestling is, "Why, Lord?"

It has been two years since that horrific year, and my grief journey has been a series of ups and downs. Along the way, the Lord showed up in ways that can only be described as miraculous. As a result, my faith has become even stronger, and I now understand more clearly that the Lord has been with me the entire time. I must admit, though, I did not always feel this way. My journey has been met with many trials, mostly due to the many lies shared by the Enemy, along with my personal life-long "flesh" struggles, especially with perfectionism.

In addition to the grace and mercy of God, what has gotten me through these past couple of years has been the patience and kindness of so many wonderful family members and friends who have allowed me to tell my story many times over. I also found a great deal of solace in hearing the triumph over grief stories of others. These stories and encounters gave me hope that I would not only learn to accept the loss of my loved ones, but that God would also leverage my personal loss for good in some capacity.

This book and journal serve as a testimony of my grief journey for others who have experienced traumatic loss, especially during the recent pandemic. I pray the humorous stories bring laughter to your life, and my story of God's miraculous transformation of sorrow into triumph brings you hope, comfort, and solace.

Since I now understand the therapeutic benefits of journaling, the journal portion of this book not only provides you insight into the emotions, truths, and lies I encountered during my grief journey, but also provides space for you to journal your personal experiences.

The resources portion of this book contains access to the churches and programs that God leveraged to help me fully accept the losses of my loved ones. I pray these resources play a pivotal role in your personal story of triumph.

Table of Contents

Introduction

T HE PURPOSE OF this book/journal is to help others who
have experienced traumatic loss, especially multiple losses of
loved ones within a short period of time. I do feel inspired by God
to write it. By sharing my personal story of loss and the phases of
grief I experienced, I pray others can find solace and hope as they
traverse their personal grief journeys.

COVID-19 was the cause of two of my losses. I know there are
other individuals who are currently grappling with the loss of multiple loved ones due to this pandemic and may feel a sense of hopelessness and despair. I want you to know you are not alone; God is
with you, even if you cannot feel His presence right now.

The first section of this book, "Our Story," contains an overview
of my life and the lives of my family members who are now with the
Lord. Please read this section carefully. God has revealed to me that

He has been preparing me all along not only for 2021, but for who I was to become in the years following.

The second section, **"2021,"** I must admit was the toughest section for me to write. It shares the details of the losses of my three immediate family members.

The third section, **"My Grief Journey: A Journal,"** chronicles my personal grief journey, including the emotions, lies and truths I experienced during each phase of this process. A Bible verse is included for reflection at the beginning of each phase, along with space for the reader to record thoughts that come to mind while reading it.

The fourth and final section, **"What I Know Now,"** summarizes the revelations that were given to me through God and through my experiences. I hope it provides you with some insights that will help you as you grieve the loss(es) of your loved one(s).

I do not know what led you to this book, nor how much pain you may be experiencing due to your loss(es). Know that you are not alone and that picking up this book was no accident. I truly pray my story provides you with comfort, hope, and peace, and strengthens your relationship with the Lord.

Our Story

Our Story

A Bit About Me

I WAS BORN IN my mama's hometown of Nashville, Tennessee in 1965. My mama and daddy met while attending Tennessee State University in Nashville together. Mama, Daddy, and I moved to Michigan in 1968 and that is where Daddy began his career at Ford Motor Company, a few years after obtaining his bachelor's in aeronautics. He joined Ford as a graduate trainee production supervisor and later transitioned to labor relations and human resources until retiring in June of 2001 at just fifty-seven years old after working thirty-three years.

My parents both accepted Christ as their Lord and Savior at a very young age as did my younger brother, Troy, and I.

I was always extremely quiet, shy, and empathetic. During my younger years and into adulthood, I always considered kindness to be the most important character trait. When I was in first grade, my teacher played the song "Somewhere Over the Rainbow" in class on the record player. It moved me so much I began to cry. I came home after school and told my parents how the song had made me feel. Daddy, who was never very good at hiding his amusement, immediately burst into laughter. I turned to Mama who was much better at maintaining her composure. She smiled and said, "That is so sweet." I remember giving Daddy a glare.

A similar story occurred when I was around five years old. Christmas was approaching and I wanted to make a gift for Mama and Daddy, so I decided I would make a Christmas tree skirt. I was so excited to be able to surprise them with a gift I made myself, without asking one of them to take me to the store to buy supplies! I found an old, ragged sheet in the closet and worked tirelessly, coloring pictures in my Christmas coloring books during the weeks leading up to Christmas. I cut out all the pictures I colored and pasted them carefully onto the sheet. Next, I found a box and some wrapping paper so I could make the gift look extra special. One evening, when Mama and Daddy were not looking, I hid my box under the Christmas tree. I could not wait to see the expressions on Mama and Daddy's faces when they opened this special surprise gift!

It was finally Christmas morning. As we were opening gifts, I told Mama and Daddy I had a gift for them and pointed to the box. They looked at me in amazement, then retrieved the box from under the tree. I waited patiently as Daddy unwrapped the gift and finally opened the box. I sat there with an angelic expression, waiting to hear "What a beautiful gift!" or "When did you have time to work on this?" Instead, all I heard was laughter from them both, followed by Daddy asking, "What is this?"

I said, "It is a tree skirt I made all by myself."

Daddy then actually fell on the floor laughing. Mama did not do much better. I was crushed! I never let them forget that day, and each time I retold the story, they would laugh just as loudly.

I believe I was a novelty to my parents because I was such a "bleeding heart." I was an advocate for anyone who was considered an underdog. When I was in fourth grade, a girl named Felicia was picked on daily at school. This bothered me, so I worked extra hard to be the best friend possible to her. I always sat next to her in the auditorium and during lunch. One day, I went home and told Mama I wanted to buy a special gift for Felicia to make her feel better. Mama took me to the store, and we picked out a necklace we both thought she would like. The next day, I gave it to Felicia, and she told me she loved it! I was the only friend she had. This made me feel happy, but also sad for her. I remember that day so vividly, and still wonder whatever became of Felicia.

My Animated Baby Brother

My brother, Troy, was born in 1969. My parents told me I would say to them, "This is my baby." I was a very protective older sister and loved my little brother so much. His birth made our family of four complete. Troy and I were polar opposites. Daddy would tell everyone I could go outside and play in the mud, wearing a white dress, making mud pies and would never get dirty. Troy, on the other hand, could just look at mud and get dirty. Troy had Mama's gift of gabbing and could talk anyone "into the ground." This did not always work to his advantage in school where he would often receive poor citizenship grades because he talked constantly.

Daddy loved to share a story with us about a car trip we took from Detroit to Nashville when Troy was just two years old (before car seat laws). Troy stood on the elevated section of the floor between the two backseats and talked during the entire car ride while I slept and read books.

Troy was also a very animated child. He had a blanket he carried with him and named "Blanket Franklin" (our family name is Franklin) and a plush tiger toy he named "Tiger Franklin." He constantly told us stories about the adventures Blanket and Tiger Franklin would take every day. In that fashion, Troy always kept us entertained. He would stand by the washer and dryer and whimper while waiting for "Blanket Franklin" to be cleaned and dried whenever Mama got tired of looking at the filth that accumulated from it being dragged around everywhere.

One of Troy's traits known by everyone close to him was that he never sugarcoated anything and was always a straight shooter, yet he still had a heart of gold and loved his family and friends. He maintained many friendships from elementary school until the end of his life. One of these good friends, Lowell, reminded me after Troy's passing of something that happened when they first transitioned from elementary school to middle school.

In elementary school, Lowell always carried a Hulk lunch box, which he loved. He and Troy always sat together to eat lunch in elementary school. After beginning middle school, Lowell continued to carry his cherished Hulk lunch box. The first day of middle school, Lowell sat down to eat his lunch and noticed Troy walking right by him to sit with some other friends. This continued for a few days until Lowell finally confronted Troy and asked why he did not want to eat lunch with him anymore. Troy looked Lowell right in the eye and said, "We are in middle school now. You better switch to a brown bag or something because if you continue to carry that Hulk lunch box, I am not eating with you!" Lowell promptly switched to a paper lunch bag the next day, and Troy resumed eating lunch with him.

While we were in elementary and middle school, Mama volunteered in the lunchroom. I do believe she did this just so she could keep an eye on Troy. Unfortunately for him, Mama's outgoing and social butterfly personality resulted in her quickly becoming friends with all our teachers and administrators as well as the principal of our school. Mama's plan seemed to work because Troy knew if he got into trouble, his teachers would simply find Mama and tell her exactly what had occurred.

Scouting and sports played major roles in Troy's life. During his younger years, Troy enjoyed skateboarding and competing in BMX competitions. I remember attending Troy's softball, basketball, and football games when he was older. He was even captain of the football team his senior year. Troy was close to six foot four (slightly shorter than Daddy) and was certainly built like a football player. He was "hard-hitting" and very protective of his teammates.

Retaliation was truly in store for anyone on the opposing team who displayed unnecessary roughness.

Troy had a terrific sense of humor into his adult years and always kept us entertained. He found joy and humor in everything. Troy loved hip-hop music. Some of his favorite artists were Run-D.M.C., Rakim, and LL Cool J. Every now and then, he would hold a one-man hip-hop "concert" for us during our living room gatherings.

After high school, Troy went on to attend Mississippi Valley State University on a football scholarship. He later transferred to Tennessee State University where he obtained a bachelor's degree in business administration. Afterwards, he worked in management positions at various companies around Nashville. Things were going well, until a major health setback changed the course of his life.

Troy was diagnosed with diabetes his freshman year of college in 1987. It was manageable; however, his health markedly declined many years after finishing college. In 2005, he returned to Detroit to live with our parents and worked locally. Complications associated with diabetes resulted in Troy having to receive dialysis treatment three times a week and ultimately led to both of his legs being amputated a few years apart.

Despite the many medical challenges that he faced throughout his life, Troy never felt sorry for himself. He was so positive about his predicament that the dialysis technicians would refer new patients, particularly young ones, to him for counsel on how to manage life while on dialysis. In his roughly fifteen years on dialysis, he never missed a treatment. He told several of his peers he loved coming to dialysis because without it, he would not be alive.

A Memorable Childhood

Our younger years consisted of the same activities as most children living in the Midwest during the 1970s. Our bikes were king. We rode all day long to visit friends or just to ride. Mama had one rule for us and that was to always be home before the streetlights came on. This was an easy rule for me to follow, but Troy always cut it too close. I remember many evenings outside with my Mama looking for Troy, and sure enough, he would fly around the corner, standing up, eyes wide as golf balls, and pedaling as hard as possible on his banana-seat bike while the streetlights illuminated his flight home. Mama would just shake her head and stare at him as he put away his bike.

Another pastime I enjoyed was sitting in the living room with my brother, listening to records, and watching my parents sing and dance together. I remember when the movie *Saturday Night Fever* was all the rage. My parents went to see the movie and I saw multiple trailers of it. We were sitting in the living room one day and I dared to tell Daddy, "You cannot dance as well as John Travolta." Why in the world did I tell him such a thing? He responded by saying, "Girl, I can dance better than John Travolta," and proceeded to show me his best disco moves with his arms and legs flying in all directions. We all laughed until we cried. Daddy always thought he was the best dancer to ever set foot on Earth.

I have many memories of building snowmen and snow caves with Troy while growing up in Michigan. Daddy would typically help us, and Mama was always quick to bring us hot chocolate so we could enjoy it in our new "snow home" or with our "snow friend."

All holidays were big events in our home, especially Christmas. Mama cooked and baked abundantly, and the decorations made our home look like a red and green forest. Once I was old enough to bake, I would typically spend an entire day baking Christmas cookies and Mama would check in on me to ensure everything was moving along without incident. On Christmas morning, our gifts filled the entire room.

Mama was a gift giver even beyond Christmas. After I had my two children, we would receive big shipments year-round from Mama that contained beautiful clothes, toys, and games for the children. She would also add a few items for Keith, my husband, and me. When my parents would visit us in Georgia, they would always argue along the way about how many gifts Mama brought, which required Daddy to use some creativity to get them to fit inside the vehicle. I later learned that during my early years, Mama sacrificed when it came to buying herself clothes to ensure Troy and I could dress nicely.

There was one activity that took precedence over all others and that was watching a Disney movie or *The Wonderful World of Disney* on our TV that contained three channels, plus UHF–on good days. Mama served as the "verbal TV guide" each morning and would let us know what was scheduled that day. If *Mary Poppins*, *Chitty Chitty Bang Bang*, or *Bedknobs and Broomsticks* were scheduled to air, we would rearrange everything; even our 6:00 p.m. family dinner time would be replanned to ensure we could eat as a family before the movie began. This was a big event in our household as our whole family would watch together.

My Loving and Humorous Mama

My mama, Marian, was born in 1942 and grew up in Nashville, Tennessee the third oldest of six siblings. She lived with her mother, father, grandmother, four sisters, and one brother. Their childhood home is still part of our family; a beautiful home, located very close to Belmont University, that has been well-maintained over the years.

Mama's family is not only large, but also loving, caring, and hilarious. I guess that is why humor was always a big part of Mama's personality. She would often tell me large families knew how to entertain each other just by sitting around talking, telling jokes, singing, and dancing. This part of Mama's childhood certainly trickled down through each generation of our family. She would share so many funny stories from her childhood with us. As I grew older, I began to realize Mama and her siblings would tell the same funny stories over and over and laugh until they cried each time, as if they were hearing them for the very first time. This is still true today. Mama was certainly an extrovert and seemed to know everyone.

When we first moved to Michigan, we lived in a small town by the name of Inkster until right before my ninth birthday. I had many friends in this town. One time, Mama thought it would be funny to dress Troy up as a girl. She dressed him up in my pink and white gingham dress, white knee-high socks, a pair of my black Mary Jane shoes, and crowned his head with one of her huge 70s-style wigs. She asked me to go get my friends and have them come over. When they arrived, she introduced Troy as our cousin Janet from Nashville. They all looked very strangely at this weird looking "girl" standing in front of them. The joke was working perfectly until Troy decided to do a karate kick and was, unfortunately, not wearing underwear. Mama laughed hysterically... I was mortified.

Troy and I loved playing games with Mama. She managed to play with us all day during the summer and still cook the most delicious meals you could ever imagine. She was a talented cook. She always told us cooking was how she showed others how much she loved them.

One of our favorite games was "Old Maid." When I was younger, I was amazed at how Mama managed to win every time we played this game. She would bend over laughing whenever I became the Old Maid. When Troy became older, he would join us in the game. That is when Mama let me in on her secret. She would bend the corner of the Old Maid card ever so slightly and somehow distract us so we would magically end up with it. Mama and I would laugh so hard when Troy would become the Old Maid repeatedly. He would cry each time, and I would hug and console him, always feeling a bit guilty.

Later, after we moved to Detroit, we met many new friends and, again, spent our days outside playing. A couple of these friends were Brian and Steve-O (a nickname for Stephen). They were brothers who lived four doors down from us. Brian was Troy's age with blonde hair and Steve-O was a couple years younger with light brown hair. I believe Troy and Brian let Steve-O hang around just because he was so funny. He actually spoke similarly to Froggy from *The Little Rascals.*

One time, Mama decided it would be nice to invite Brian and Steve-O to attend church with us. Steve-O was no older than five at the time. Everything went smoothly until the holy Communion elements were passed around. Steve-O, who had evidently never partaken in holy Communion, took them before Mama could stop him and exclaimed in his deep, raspy voice as he leaned back casually, "I think I like this church. Have a little snack. Drink a little juice." We all laughed until it hurt, which was a bit embarrassing at church, but since Mama was laughing so hard, we knew it was okay.

Mama was always concerned that we would lose our self-identity since there were only a few African-American families in our neighborhood. One time, Brian, Steve-O, and Troy were playing cowboys in the backyard. Mama decided to take them lemonade and cookies, as she did regularly. She walked outside and placed the tray on the patio table. While walking back inside, she heard Troy exclaim, "Let us White boys head over there!" Mama simply came back into the house and told me what she heard. "I believe Troy thinks he is White," she said. I just listened to her, not knowing if this was true or not. She immediately walked outside and asked Troy if he could come inside for a moment. When he arrived, she asked, "Troy, do you know you are Black?" He responded, "Yes, I know I am." She looked perplexed and repeated to him what she overheard. Troy looked at her and said "Steve-O and I are wearing white cowboy hats and Brian is wearing a black one. That is why I said what I did." Mama felt really silly, but also laughed really hard. Troy went back outside to play, and Mama called her family in Nashville to tell the story to everyone who picked up their phone.

Mama spent a lot of time volunteering at the Presbyterian church we attended in our neighborhood and cooking food for every ill person or shut-in she came across. She also worked as an employee at the Detroit Metro Convention and Visitors Bureau for over thirty years after I finished high school. She developed many lasting friendships from her years at the Bureau and seemed to make friends with everyone who walked through the door.

Mama also was a Cub Scout den leader for my brother and a Girl Scout leader for me. In addition, she served as a deacon and elder at our church and was a member of a few social clubs. Later in life, she joined a women's bowling league and was recognized for her outstanding bowling abilities, which surprised us and her.

Scouting played a major role in our family. I continued in Girl Scouts through the level of Cadette (middle school) while Troy continued in Boy Scouts and was just one badge away from becoming an Eagle Scout when sports got in the way.

Music also played a major role in Mama's life. I remember listening to what Daddy referred to as "elevator music" on a regular basis. Mama would also regularly croon to anything by Frankie Valli. If I close my eyes, I can hear her singing, "You're just too good to be true. Can't take my eyes off of you." Frank Sinatra and Al Green were also a couple of her favorite singers. As you can tell, her tastes in music varied broadly. Music played a major role and still does in the lives of Mama's siblings and my cousins, as well. Whether singing at their church or just at family gatherings, I cannot recall a time when I did not hear someone vocalizing within my family.

Mama had a servant's heart and always put others before herself. With her humor and infectious laugh, she made life, holidays, birthdays, family gatherings, and other special occasions extra special.

My Intelligent and Engaging Daddy

My daddy, Harry, was born in 1943 and grew up in the beautiful valley of Roanoke, Virginia along with his mama, his daddy, and younger sister, Joan. While growing up, I did not fully comprehend the beauty of Roanoke. It was not until I had to fly back to attend my aunt's funeral in 2000 that I was able to fully appreciate the majestic mountains surrounding the city. My granddaddy was a successful entrepreneur and was able to provide a very comfortable quality of life for his family, including having a beautiful brick home built when Daddy was very young. This was certainly very rare for an African-American family during the pre-civil rights era.

Daddy was one of the smartest people I ever met. Once, he told me he began reading the encyclopedia when he was just three years old. He was the president of the student council in eight grade and played football at Lucy Addison High School. Daddy introduced me to the love of reading and books at a very young age. He also introduced me to my favorite hobby of miniature dollhouse collecting, a hobby I still enjoy today.

Although he grew up during a very stoic period, Daddy was a very loving and engaged parent. Some of my fondest childhood memories are of me sitting on his lap while watching movies. Watching movies is still one of my favorite past times. Daddy also had a rule that my brother and I could not go to bed without exchanging "I love you" with him and kissing him good night. Considering Daddy's stature of over six feet four inches and his high level of intelligence, it was truly out of the ordinary for him to humble himself to a child's level and be such a loving and attentive father.

Daddy was also a colorful storyteller. He would tell us some of the most outrageous stories about growing up in Roanoke. I dismissed them as fiction, created just to entertain my brother and me. I thought of him as a regular Edward Bloom from *Big Fish*, but I later realized most of the stories were true, or at least mostly true. A couple of the most entertaining stories were about his albino cousins (stage names of Eko and Iko) who were kidnapped from their Virginia home and forced to become circus performers without compensation for many years. Other stories included adventures throughout Virginia with friends and the many antics that occurred along the way. This is one reason why Daddy has always enjoyed movies like *The Goonies* and *Stand by Me*. These are still a couple of my favorites and my children's favorites, as well.

A very humorous story Daddy shared was told to him by his grandmother. She told him about a young man who would periodically hop on the train as a stowaway when it stopped in his hometown of Roanoke, ride it to the next town, then jump off the train when it returned to Roanoke (a common practice amongst young folks in Roanoke at the time). Well, one time, the young man hopped on the train, but on the way back, the train did not stop in Roanoke. In fact, the train did not stop for several days. The young man could be seen by the townspeople, waving his hand from the train as it passed back and forth past Roanoke until the train finally stopped in Roanoke and the man was able to go home. Daddy admits he believes his grandmother made up this story just to scare him into staying off those trains.

During my last two years of high school, Daddy took me to the library to explore majors and careers. He always told us we could become anything we wanted with a college degree and hard work. From a young age, he told us he would pay for our college and would support any major we chose but expected us to graduate. He later told me that since I enjoyed math and science so much and did so well in school, I should consider a challenging career such as engineering, medicine, or law. He also told me (this was around 1980) he believed industrial engineering was a great career to research because, eventually, most companies would require engineers of this type who could improve efficiency and reduce cost. His prediction certainly was realized, considering the tremendous expansion of industrial engineering over the years. Well, I listened to Daddy and went on to obtain a bachelor's in industrial and systems engineering from the University of Michigan (Dearborn, MI campus) in 1987, followed by an MBA. These two degrees opened doors to a successful career with a Fortune 500 company for close to thirty-six years.

In addition to his career at Ford Motor Company, Daddy served in many leadership positions at our church and in the community. He was a Cub Scout leader and Scoutmaster for the Boy Scouts of America for nine years. He took his scouts on trips down the Rifle River in Michigan and to Washington DC, which resulted in their appearance on the front of a scouting magazine. He also coached my brother's little league softball and basketball teams. He served on the board of directors of the YMCA and the Detroit Tennessee State University Alumni Association Foundation (he chartered this foundation, which provides scholarship grants to Detroit-area students who attend Tennessee State University) and the Southfield Kappa Alpha Psi Fraternity Foundation, which, since its inception, has provided over $800,000 in scholarship grants to Detroit-area students.

Daddy was initiated into the Southfield Alumni Chapter of Kappa Alpha Psi Fraternity in 1988. Kappa Alpha Psi is a historically Black fraternity and Daddy served in various positions, including executive-level roles, both local and on the national board. He also received many awards during his tenure. He truly loved the Kappa organization and was considered a mentor, confidant, counselor, role model, and friend to all within the organization who knew him. Michael, Daddy's dear friend and fellow Kappa, who you will hear more about in the next chapter, recently shared with me that Daddy never sought any position within the Kappa organization but was always asked to do so. He emphasized how this speaks volumes regarding his character.

Daddy also held a number of leadership positions within the church including deacon, elder, treasurer, and chairman of the finance committee. He is a life member of Lucy Addison High School class of 1961, Tennessee State University Alumni Association, and Kappa Alpha Psi Fraternity, Inc.

During the summer, my family would travel to Roanoke to visit my grandparents, aunt, uncle, and cousins. We always had an enjoyable time and would sometimes visit The Roanoke Star, known as the Mill Mountain Star. Daddy loved taking us around town to show us his former schools and point out some of the landmarks from his many stories. We also enjoyed visiting with our cousins. They were funny and entertaining.

Next, we would travel to Nashville to visit my grandparents, great-grandmother, aunts, uncles and cousins. We would often take the scenic route along the Blue Ridge Parkway. The majestic mountains, streaming waters, and overall serenity stirred my soul so much that I still have a love for mountains and nature today. Since there were no cell phones during those times, our Nashville family would hold a vigil at my grandparents' home until we arrived. I have early memories of pulling into the driveway of our grandparents' home, seeing my cousins watch us pull into the driveway from the front door while yelling, "They are here!" and running to the back door to greet us when we arrived. Regardless of how late we arrived, Grandma always had a hot dinner waiting for us, which included Daddy's favorite dessert, blackberry cobbler. Daddy definitely had a sweet tooth.

One of those trips to Roanoke and Nashville occurred shortly after Daddy decided he loved country music, especially Kenny Rogers and Willie Nelson. I can still recite every word of "The Gambler." Other songs Daddy insisted on singing loudly during our drive were "Always on My Mind," "To All the Girls I've Loved Before," and "Mammas, Don't Let Your Babies Grow Up to Be Cowboys". Daddy adored any song by Glen Campbell with one of his favorites being "Wichita Lineman." He also loved Motown and rhythm and blues. Singing and dancing like The Temptations was one of his favorite forms of entertainment for us.

Daddy also enjoyed western movies and TV shows. I remember watching *Gunsmoke* and *McCloud* with him, along with other shows. He adored *Lonesome Dove* and was so excited when the miniseries premiered in 1989. Daddy enjoyed hunting, gun collecting, golf, leathercrafts, rug crafting, books, and the list goes on and on. He constantly kept himself busy while maintaining a career and spending quality time with family.

Daddy and I worked together to plan our family vacations. In addition to visiting our family in Virginia and Tennessee, one vacation that stands out is a trip we took right before my fourteenth birthday with our travel trailer through Canada in August 1979. Daddy had taught me how to read maps years prior, so I served as the designated navigator to ensure we stayed on course. Some of our key stops included Toronto, Quebec City, Montreal, Prince Edwards Island, and Moncton, New Brunswick. Our ultimate destination was Halifax, Nova Scotia. One of my favorite stops along the way was Peggy's Cove, Nova Scotia. I can still see the rocky shore, the towering lighthouse, and hear the ocean water as it washed against the rocks. Peggy's Cove felt like heaven on Earth to me. When Troy got older, he and Daddy would often go on camping trips together. Mama and I would stay home and spend some quality girl time together.

A love for the Lord, a sense of humor, hard work, a love for sports and music, academic achievement, generosity, kindness, love, the importance of a college education, and valuing family and friendships are the primary lessons I learned while growing up with my family. These are also the lessons I brought into my marriage to my devoted husband for close to thirty years and our two wonderful children (now young adults). I certainly did live a "charmed life," as Daddy would say, and it was all due to the loving family in which I was born. What a blessing to be raised in such a household with parents who were so devoted and caring.

2021

2021

AS 2020 DREW to an end, we were so excited about a new COVID vaccine that was close to becoming available to the public. Like so many, we had been disconnected from family and friends for far too long. We especially missed seeing Mama, Daddy, and Troy. We had not met in person since the end of 2019, when we travelled to Detroit to visit them the day after Christmas. We all knew 2021 was going to be an exciting and wonderful year.

Keith and I had visions of spending summers in Detroit and renting a home on the lake in one of the surrounding suburbs since I had retired at the end of 2020 and Keith's job could, for the most part, be worked remotely. Daddy, Mama, and Troy could stay with us if they wanted. If not, we could visit them at their home as often as we liked. We were especially excited because Troy had not travelled since he began dialysis treatments many years prior. This would provide him with a welcome change of environment without leaving the Metro-Detroit area. How could we have ever fathomed 2021 would turn out to be just the opposite...

Mama and Troy's Health Decline

Daddy, Mama, and I mutually agreed we should not visit in-person during Christmas 2020 because the risk was too great. After all, considering Troy's underlying health conditions, the last thing any of us wanted to do was expose him to COVID. So, we connected via Zoom on Christmas day to share the excitement of opening our presents. Troy was a little "under the weather," so our family of four connected with just Mama and Daddy.

A few days later, Mama and Daddy told us Troy was in the hospital and there was a chance he had COVID due to his high temperature and other symptoms. He was admitted on January 2. Of course, the doctors could not be certain he had COVID until after a test had been run. The test results confirmed our biggest fear... Troy had tested positive. We were all concerned, considering his fragile condition, but I knew he would be just fine. After all, everything always worked out for me and God had not failed me yet.

Troy spoke on the phone constantly while he was in the hospital. He called our family members in Nashville, as well as Mama, Daddy and us. Troy kept us in stitches as he complained about the bland food he was restricted to eating due to his diabetes. He told everyone he phoned that the first thing he planned to do once he was released from the hospital was eat a Baconator burger from Wendy's. He had seen the advertisements everywhere before he was admitted, but he had not yet tried one. He also indicated he wanted more snacks than the hospital staff was willing to bring him, most likely because the hospital was overrun with COVID patients at the time. I immediately ordered snacks, a warm blanket, and a few more items to be shipped to him.

Unfortunately, Troy never had a chance to consume any of the snacks. Due to his claustrophobia, a few days after being admitted, Troy began removing and tugging at his CPAP device while he was asleep. As a result, he was given the option of transitioning from his CPAP device to a ventilator and to be given medication that would keep him in a semi-comatose state. He opted for this transition.

Over the next few days, Troy's condition began to worsen. The worst part was that I was in Georgia during this time. Daddy said I should remain in Georgia because of the COVID restrictions at the hospital, which limited access to the ICU. He also said he and Mama had begun to experience COVID symptoms. Fortunately, Daddy only experienced loss of taste and a bad cough. Mama had a fever and began experiencing flu-like symptoms and was quite lethargic. She spoke on the phone regularly to her family in Nashville and with us. We tried desperately to convince her to let Daddy take her to the hospital and Daddy did, as well, but she did not want to go without showering first and she did not want to be transported by ambulance.

Finally, on Sunday, January 10, I convinced her to let Daddy take her to the hospital. She said she would wait to go on Monday because she was feeling a little better and was even able to shower. Late on Sunday night, Daddy went in to check on Mama and she was incoherent and mumbling to herself. He immediately realized something was wrong and called 911. Later that evening, he sent me a text to let me know Mama was in the hospital. I felt better knowing she would be under a doctor's care. I called Daddy to let him know I could act as the primary contact for the doctors and nurses on Mama's behalf if he preferred, since he was still dealing with Troy. I knew this would be too much for one individual to manage. Daddy accepted my assistance.

I honestly had no idea of what I was getting myself into, the emotional strain this would cause nor the guilt that would consume me down the road. Per a discussion with the ER team, I was not able to contact the admitting nurse until 5:30 a.m. on Monday. I called the nurse's station right at 5:30 a.m. and Mama's admitting nurse was paged. A sweet nurse named Jessica picked up the phone. She was so patient and kind and slowly and clearly shared Mama's vitals with me. I felt ill. Since Mama was feeling better on Sunday, I just knew she would be fine within a couple of days and would be discharged.

Instead, Jessica shared with me that Mama was in the ICU on a ventilator because her oxygen level was less than 25 percent when she was admitted, her blood pressure was not stable, and there were a host of additional medical issues impacting her. However, Jessica was very hopeful and indicated we just needed to be patient and wait for the ventilator and medicines to work. She also told me Mama's doctor would reach out to us later in the day to provide an even more thorough update. Once the doctor called, I conferenced Daddy in so he could hear the conversation, along with Keith and myself. The doctor was not nearly as hopeful as Jessica. She was concerned about Mama's diabetes and her age on top of her other medical issues caused by COVID. We all felt very deflated and fearful after that call.

In the meantime, Troy's condition was about the same. His oxygen level was still very low, but he was stable. Mama's condition was slowly improving, especially her oxygen level. Having both Mama and Troy in the hospital in such fragile states was extremely difficult and emotional for our family. Daddy and I spent the next few days contacting Mama and Troy's respective nurses for periodic updates and waiting for updates from their respective doctors as they were both in different hospitals. Sleep and nourishment took a back seat during this time for me. I was constantly on edge and prayed consistently for God to restore Mama and Troy's health. I also spent a lot of time updating Mama's family via text and phone calls, depending on the nature of the information I needed to share. I asked them to pray for Mama and Troy, as well. They did so and also reached out to their respective churches and friends to ask them to pray.

A Shocking Phone Call

A few days after Mama was admitted, on the evening of Thursday, January 14, I received a phone call from Mama's hospital. I was very nervous while answering and braced myself for terrible news, but when I picked up the phone, I heard Mama's voice on the other end before I could even answer. Jessica was with her, and they explained that Mama had accidentally removed her ventilator. Since her body responded so well, she was allowed to keep it off and only use a CPAP device. I could tell Mama was tired and her voice was quite raspy, but she "talked up a storm!" It was so comforting to hear her voice and know she was comfortable. She told me how much she loved Jessica and that she could not wait to get home. I was in shock and excited at the same time. Finally, one of them would be leaving the hospital soon!

Keith joined in on the conversation. I later found out Jessica had requested to be assigned to Mama's area in the ICU during her shifts so she could be with her. They became quite close. After we spoke, I thanked God for this miracle and immediately told our children and contacted Mama's family to share the great news with them. Over the next few days, Mama continued to improve and was moved out of the ICU. She was also transitioned from the CPAP to a portable oxygen tank. She started doing some breathing and physical exercises to enable her to be discharged.

While Mama was improving, Troy's condition was getting worse. Daddy called me a couple days later to inform me that Troy's oxygen level was dropping, one of his lungs had collapsed and the doctor did not expect him to make it through the night. My heart sank. I updated everyone and, as usual, asked them to pray for Troy's health to improve. The next day, I called Daddy to ask for an update. He contacted the doctor and called me back to inform me that Troy was stable for the time being. I breathed a sigh of relief.

Mama was still doing well and calling relatives to update them. We talked at least a few times a day. Mama also called Daddy quite a few times to check in and make sure he was taking care of things at the house properly.

Devastating News

On Wednesday, January 20, Daddy called me with the worst news I had ever received up to that point in my life...Troy had passed away. I was in shock. I asked him how he was doing, and he said he was "fine." After our conversation, I immediately called to update our family members. Everyone was so sad. It is strange to receive news like that and still know the world continues as it was before. There is no fanfare before you receive the news nor fanfare afterwards. My funny, generous little brother was gone, but life continued.

We were reluctant to tell Mama because she was doing so well. Daddy called to tell her, and I spoke with her later that day. She was doing fine and told me Troy had so many health issues that she had not expected him to be able to survive. When Mama told me she was doing fine, I believed her because Mama always shared her feelings. She was an open book; however, I worried so much about Daddy because he always kept his feelings locked up inside. I never saw him cry in my entire life, nor even come close to crying. Mama said she was concerned about Daddy, as well. I told her I would check on him regularly. When I called him later, he was cleaning out Troy's things. It took him a few days, but I know he appreciated the distraction. Daddy had always been very organized, so being able to clean Troy's room and haul items to the church and trash took his mind off Troy... for a while at least.

In the meantime, the lead doctor for Mama came into her room while I was speaking with her. He just wanted to find out her resuscitation preferences. I was a bit confused, but he explained to me that COVID patients often experience relapses. He reassured me he did not currently have any concerns and that this was a routine question. Mama indicated that she wanted to be sustained with a ventilator if required and she also wanted to be resuscitated if necessary. I finished the call and hung up. Later, Mama called to tell me to not let that doctor scare me and that she felt just fine and expected to be heading home in a few days.

A Turn of Events

Later in the week, I had not heard from Mama one morning after speaking with her regularly each day, so I decided to call her. My call to her cell phone went to voicemail. This happened a few times. I decided to call the nurse's station and was told she was moved back into ICU because her oxygen level dropped. I could not believe what I was hearing. I just lost my brother a few days ago and now Mama was back in the ICU. I called Daddy to inform him. "Tell your mama she cannot leave me here alone," was his reply which cut to my very core. I felt it was my responsibility to ensure Mama stayed alive at all costs, but her condition deteriorated daily, and she was placed back on a ventilator. My frantic regular calls to obtain updates from the nurses and waiting on updates from her doctors started all over again. I resumed my sleepless nights and regiment of not eating or drinking. The only time I ate anything was when Keith would force me to eat. He was not only concerned about Mama, but very concerned about me, as well.

A few days later, on the morning of Tuesday, January 26, Mama's doctor asked me if I wanted her to facilitate a Zoom call with Mama and anyone else who wanted to attend. Later that day, Daddy, Keith, and I joined the call, but I honestly do not know if that helped Mama or us. She looked so frail and could not speak because she was on a ventilator. We said encouraging things to her and told her how much we loved her. We also told her to be strong and let her know we were praying for her. I noticed a tear rolling down Mama's face which was so difficult for us to see, especially since she could not speak. The doctor called me later to chat. I believe she was checking to ensure I was okay as she was aware of the loss of my brother. I truly appreciated her call.

By Wednesday, January 27, Mama's doctor called me to let me know she was experiencing a lot of difficulties. She was not only on a ventilator, but various devices and medications to sustain her life, especially her blood pressure, which had dropped quite low before the medication was administered. Her doctor said very calmly and slowly, "Pray for your mother." I thanked the doctor and immediately went to work updating all the family members and asking them to pray for Mama.

Saying Goodbye to Mama

That evening, for the first time in a while, I slept very deeply. I awakened around 4:30 a.m. in a panic and happened to check my cell phone. I noticed Mama's hospital called me twice around 1:30 a.m. on the morning of January 28, but I evidently slept right through both calls. I immediately called the nurse's station to ask about Mama. She gave me a brief update but indicated the doctor would call me shortly. The lead doctor called to inform me that Mama coded twice during the night, which meant we are dealing with a very different scenario. I told him I understood and reminded him of Mama's resuscitation wishes. He said he understood, shared Mama's vitals, and told me they were watching her very closely.

Later in the morning, the doctor who facilitated the Zoom call a couple days prior called me to let me know Mama's condition had not improved. Her speaking manner was very calm, and I could tell she was trying to select her words very carefully.

"Are you trying to tell me I should let my mother go peacefully?" I asked.

"Yes," she responded, "but it is very hard for loved ones to hear those words."

We understood clearly that Mama wanted to be resuscitated, but at the same time, none of us wanted her to be in pain or discomfort with no ability to communicate this to us. The doctor explained that Mama was on multiple medications and other forms of life support, not just the ventilator. In addition, it was difficult to assess just how close to death Mama was at the time. The doctor was not able to assess her cognitive abilities and there was a very good chance the lack of oxygen flow through her brain when she had coded impacted her cognitive abilities. Knowing all of this, the doctor suggested we consider taking her off just one medication to see how her body responded. The doctor ensured I clearly understood there was a possibility Mama would pass away if she was truly that close to death. I told the doctor I first wanted to speak with my father to find out his opinion, so I called Daddy and told him about our discussion. He said that Mama appeared to be at the same stage as Troy right before he passed away. He agreed that one of the medications should be removed. I immediately called the doctor and shared our decision.

Since there was a very good chance Mama would not pull through, we all decided it would be best to speak to her on the phone and say our final goodbyes. She was mostly unconscious, but her nurse, Kate, told us there was a very good possibility Mama could hear us since hearing is one of the last senses to go when someone is close to death. She also told us she would not leave Mama's side and would hold her hand the entire time. Even though I was so sad at the time, I did pause long enough to realize that God provided Mama with the best intake nurse in Jessica and the best nurse near the end of her life in Kate. They are both two of the most loving, compassionate individuals I have ever encountered. Who could have guessed that several months down the road I would have a chance to meet these two wonderful ladies in-person while facing the loss of yet another loved one?

Keith and I spoke to Mama first. I told Mama how much I loved her through tears. I was crying so hard I know I sounded like a child, and I certainly felt like one. How do you choose the final words to share with someone who has had such a tremendous impact on your life and has loved you unconditionally? How do you tell your mama, who might be leaving this earth, how much you love her? I told her she was the best mother anyone could have, that I would miss her, but that we would all be okay. I told her we would take care of Daddy and ask him to move in with us. Keith was next and was crying just as hard as me. My mother had become his mother after his own mother passed away in a similar fashion in 2013. Mama and Keith spoke every day on the phone for at least an hour. He loved her so much.

Finally, we let Kate know we were going to hang up so Daddy could call and speak to Mama. About fifteen minutes after our call to Mama, the lead doctor called to inform me that Mama passed away within seven minutes of the medication being paused. I was not surprised, but I was numb. I called Daddy right away to update him. Daddy said he was going to have Mama cremated because she never expressed her final wishes. Troy was cremated, as well, and had shared his desire to be cremated with Daddy many years prior. Next, Daddy and I split up the dire duty of calling family members and friends to inform them of Mama's passing. Hearing that Mama was gone was tough but calling her friends and family to tell them was almost just as tough, especially after just losing Troy. Fortunately, Mama's eldest sister, Cil, had been helping me all along with keeping the other family members updated. She was the first person I called after Daddy. She contacted Mama's other siblings to inform them of her passing. I called a few of Mama's friends and some other family members.

The next few days, I spent my time feeling somewhere between strong and numb, maybe a bit of both. I know God was certainly with me because I never could have gotten through those days on my own. I know others were concerned about me because I did not fall apart. To be honest, I was concerned about myself. I knew if I did not take time to grieve, I would definitely fall apart one day.

During the night of Saturday, January 30, just two days after Mama passed away, I tossed and turned and could not sleep. I awakened on Sunday morning and realized what was bothering me. Since Mama had not expressed a desire to be cremated, I did not believe she should be. Also, having her cremated, placed in an urn, and leaving her in the house in Detroit seemed so sad and it would also result in her family members in Nashville not having any form of closure. Daddy and I did plan on having a memorial service for Mama and Troy, but it would be held in Detroit. And since COVID was still on the rise, we did not know when the service would be held nor if it was a wise decision to have family members travel to the service. I decided to call Daddy and express my concern. I told him I wanted to have a graveside service for Mama in Nashville and that I would handle all the arrangements. I wanted her to be buried in the cemetery where Grandma, Granddaddy, and her eldest sister, Roslyn, were buried.

I assumed he would try to reason with me to opt for cremation since it would be quick and simple, but he did not. He told me he understood and shared the phone number of his fraternity brother who owned the funeral home that was coordinating the cremation in Detroit, but also indicated that there was a chance Mama's remains were already cremated over the weekend. I immediately contacted the funeral director. He told me that the crematorium was closed on Sundays, so Mama's remains had not yet been cremated. I told him I wanted her remains flown to Nashville and I planned to have an interment service for her there. He told me that would not be a problem and asked me to provide him with the name of the funeral home in Nashville I planned on using. I thanked him and called my Uncle George, Mama's brother, in Nashville who knows everyone. I explained my dilemma and he immediately gave me the name of a funeral home to use but told me he would first call and speak with the director of the funeral home to explain what was needed. By Monday, I had arranged for Mama's remains to be flown to Nashville by Wednesday, February 3, in time for an interment service in Nashville on Saturday, February 6.

Later that Sunday, I spoke with Daddy. He told me he was having a moment while his voice was cracking and that earlier he had called one of his fraternity brothers who is a pastor to ask him to pray for him and to basically reassure him that everything would be fine. Daddy said they spoke for a long time, and he felt much better afterwards; however, Daddy said something that concerned me. "Now that your mama and brother are gone, there is no reason for me to be around," he said. This scared me so much, especially to hear Daddy's voice cracking and to know he was all alone in the house in Detroit. I attempted to comfort Daddy, eventually said "goodbye," and hung up the phone. I immediately told Keith that we needed to get to Detroit as quickly as possible because I was concerned about Daddy's emotional state. Keith simply said, "Okay." I suggested we drive to Detroit the day after the memorial service for Mama.

The service for Mama was beautiful. All our family in Nashville attended. Everyone wore masks and the doors to the mausoleum were kept open because of the rise in COVID. My Uncle Bruce officiated the service (on his birthday) and we all quickly embraced before leaving. It was wonderful to see everyone and to be reminded of how blessed we are to have so many loving family members, despite our recent losses. We dropped our son back off at college and spent the night in Cincinnati, Ohio before driving to Detroit the next day.

Spending Time with Daddy

We arrived in Detroit around 1:30 p.m. on Super Bowl Sunday and planned to stay for about a week. Daddy was so happy to see us, especially since we planned to stay with him at the house as opposed to a hotel, per his insistence. We knew the noise and laughter of the three of us gave him hope and lifted his spirits. Keith immediately started cooking meals for the week as he has always been the primary cook and is excellent at it. Brooke and I started sorting through Mama's things right after we arrived. I told Daddy to not touch anything because I wanted to go through everything myself. After three days of sorting through Mama's items, we shipped at least three large boxes of special apparel items, many of them new to our family in Nashville. Daddy must have hauled over twenty bags of items to the church, and we shipped one box to our home in Georgia. During the week, we also found time to watch movies with Daddy, play some board games we brought with us, and to just talk.

Daddy hired an attorney in Michigan to address some open items regarding Troy's Estate. I accompanied Daddy to meet with the attorney. The drive there and back gave me some alone time with Daddy to really find out how he was doing. "Well, at least it no longer feels like I am in a nightmare," he said. He told me that when Troy and Mama first died, it felt unreal and like he was in a nightmare. I also told him he concerned me when I spoke with him the previous Sunday because I thought he was considering taking his own life. He said I did not have to worry about that and that he could handle emotional pain. It just takes time. He told me that what he meant to say was that he always prayed that the Lord would take Mama and Troy first because he was concerned that they would have a difficult time if he passed first, mainly due to Troy's ailments. He did not want to leave Mama with the burden of taking care of Troy. He was also concerned about Mama's diabetes. He said he was not ready to go until the Lord said it was time for him to go. I felt much better. I also asked Daddy if he would consider moving in with us. He said that his life was in Detroit, and he wanted to remain in his home. I asked him to at least consider an extended stay, maybe during the summer, and he promised to think about it.

The following Sunday, we had a great dinner in honor of Valentine's Day. A snowstorm was forecasted to move in later that evening, so we left in the afternoon, spent the night in Cincinnati (south of the forecasted storm), and headed back home to Georgia on Monday. I have to admit, it was great being back home. Being at home at least physically removed us from the sorrow we felt in Detroit, especially being in a home, once full of conversation and laughter, that was now so quiet. However, I could not help but think of Daddy alone after losing everyone in his household.

During the following weeks, I made it my personal responsibility to ensure Daddy was happy and to fill in the void left by the passing of Mama and Troy. Daddy and I spoke on the phone every day. This was very unusual because Daddy and I spoke about once every other week prior to Mama and Troy passing. We were the introverts compared to Mama and Troy who talked all the time and could easily carry a conversation by themselves. Daddy told me after Mama passed away that interacting with people seemed so different because in the past, he could just "fade into the background" and let Mama do all the talking. Now, he was required to help keep the conversation going.

Daddy, Keith, and I, with input from our family in Nashville, decided that the Saturday of Easter weekend would be the perfect day for a double memorial service for Mama and Troy at the church they attended in Detroit, Westminster Presbyterian Church of Detroit[1]. Many of the members at Westminster[1] previously attended my childhood church, Calvin Presbyterian, before it closed. During the weeks leading up to the service, I focused on planning the service with assistance from the pastor of the church (Pastor Karen, as she was affectionately called). Not only was Pastor Karen very good at assisting with planning, she also provided a great deal of comfort for me and let me know she was available for us.

The service for Mama and Troy was beautiful. Many of our family members from Nashville attended and the Kappa Alpha Psi fraternity brothers greeted us as we walked into the church and were well-represented in the pews. In addition to scripture readings and song selections by family members, Keith, Daddy, and I spoke at the service. One funny story is that the night before the service, Keith, Daddy, and I were discussing the service and attempting to agree on how much time each of us needed. Keith and I were very forthcoming with the comments we planned to discuss, but Daddy would not share his comments. He told us to take as much time as needed and he would adjust to ensure the three of us remained within the twenty-five minutes I assigned to our portion of the service.

Well, Keith and I did go over quite a bit. In fact, everything took much longer than planned, so the expectation was that Daddy would adjust his talk. Daddy did just the opposite! He spoke for twenty-five minutes by himself, but I must admit, he told some of the funniest stories and delivered his discussion points flawlessly. Daddy had always been a great speaker. He spoke like a Baptist pastor that day, and I was so proud of him. During his talk, he took the time to share that I was one of the kindest people he knew, but the most moving portion of his talk was when he said that Keith was more of a son than a son-in-law. Keith was blown away because Daddy had never shared that with him in the past. In addition, Keith never had a strong father figure in his life and always considered Daddy to be his father. Hearing this not only had a dramatic impact on him that day, but has had a profound impact on the man he has become. He speaks of that often and what it meant to hear those words.

We returned to Georgia a few days later and resumed talking to Daddy daily. I knew these daily talks and daily worrying were not sustainable and I sensed that Daddy did, as well, but for the time, they would continue. Little did we know, God had a different plan.

Troy's Legacy

Not too long after Troy passed, Daddy called to tell me about an encounter he had at Troy's dialysis clinic. Daddy decided to donate Troy's wheelchairs and a few other items to the clinic. He expected to simply drop the items off and leave; however, the supervisor of the clinic was on the phone and saw Daddy. She motioned for Daddy to wait as she hung up the phone and went to the back of the clinic. She quickly emerged along with seven or eight technicians who worked in the clinic and had known Troy. Daddy said they were all sobbing uncontrollably, each taking turns telling him what Troy meant to them and how much they missed him. Troy always took time to give everyone who worked at the clinic Christmas and birthday gifts, as well as other tokens. He would listen to their problems and offer advice when asked, despite his own challenges. Daddy was deeply moved and had no idea Troy had impacted the staff at the clinic in such an overwhelming manner.

I also had an incident that occurred following Troy's passing. I decided to contact the *Detroit Free Press* and submit an article and pictures of Mama and Troy after their passing. The paper was running a special obituary section featuring COVID victims. A week or so after submitting the article, one of the editors contacted me to share an e-mail from a physical therapist who worked with Troy. She wanted me to know that Troy was always hopeful and optimistic, and indicated his progress during their sessions was remarkable. She mentioned she was currently working as a physical therapist in Florida and used Troy's therapy videos to help her other patients.

This truly warmed my heart and made me feel good knowing Troy was still having a positive impact on the lives of many others.

A Moment of Peace

A few weeks after the memorial service in Detroit, my cousin, Janet, called from Nashville to let me know she was planning an eighty-first birthday celebration for her mom, my Aunt Cil (COVID had squashed the eightieth birthday celebration), for the beginning of June and she really wanted all of us, including Daddy, to attend. I spoke with Daddy and he indicated he would. Janet was elated as she had grown up without a father in her life and had always considered Daddy to be a father figure to her. Janet also always held a special place in Daddy's heart.

We were all excited about meeting Daddy in Nashville for the birthday celebration weekend. I booked the four of us and Daddy in two adjoining rooms at the Gaylord Opryland, one of our favorite hotels. We had so much fun attending family gatherings and spending time with Daddy. We also decided to visit the new National Museum of African American Music that had recently opened. Considering the love of music we all shared, we were excited to visit. Daddy truly enjoyed it and took time to point out the different artists and shared some of his personal stories with the four of us.

Daddy left Nashville a day earlier than us. It was a bit sad escorting him out of the hotel and hugging him goodbye, but we were so glad we had that special time together. The four of us headed back home to Georgia the following day.

We decided to drive back to Detroit to visit with Daddy for a few days over Father's Day weekend. We had never been out of town for Father's Day because Keith and Brooke typically attended a father/daughter dance, but we all decided we wanted to be with Daddy instead and had a great time in Detroit. The first day we arrived, Daddy and I both decided to sit down and review his succession plan, will, healthcare directive and other important matters in detail, and he showed me how to access all of his safes. We actually laughed the entire time and, for some reason, felt very relaxed. Daddy doubled over in laughter when I tried repeatedly to open one of his safes and could not do so. He always teased me about being an engineer and having difficulty operating certain mechanical devices. I would remind him that I am an industrial engineer, not a mechanical engineer. The strange thing about both of us deciding to review Daddy's estate plan was that he had been sending me an encrypted file containing his succession plan each year since 2001. I would always tell him he was going to live forever and I would read it when I needed to do so, but for some reason, I felt it was important to do so during that visit. Daddy did, as well.

On Saturday, we took him to Greenfield Village and Henry Ford Museum, one of his favorite museums. I had not attended the venue since I was very young and Daddy had not attended for many years. We spent the entire day walking around. Daddy enjoyed sharing personal stories and pointing out objects and structures. The next day was Fathers' Day, so we all went out to eat an early dinner. We also took pictures and lavished Daddy and Keith with gifts. It was such a great day.

A couple of days later, we were in the driveway, all packed up and ready to head back home. Daddy was pulling weeds from his garden when he looked at us with a strange expression. I felt chilled and could not figure out why. Keith felt the same way. After hugging and kissing Daddy, we said goodbye and headed home.

Daddy's Decline

A couple of weeks later, we were all in California on a vacation we had planned a year prior with three other family members and a friend of Austin's. We had tried to get Daddy to come with us, but he preferred to stay at home. On Wednesday, July 7, Keith got a call on his cell phone from Daddy's next-door neighbor. She was with a police officer and indicated the officer wanted to speak with me. He told me Daddy had fallen while he was in the basement, but he had been able to call 911. An ambulance and the officer arrived at the same time. Thankfully, Daddy's next-door neighbor ran out with a key to the house to let everyone inside before they could break down the door.

The officer said Daddy was coherent when he first arrived but was slurring his words. Once he was placed on the stretcher, he lost consciousness. I thanked the officer and called the hospital to obtain additional information. The doctor told me Daddy was not conscious and he had a severe brain hemorrhage. They would not know his prognosis until additional tests were run. After a few conversations with the doctor, I realized I needed to quickly fly to Detroit to be with Daddy. I arranged a flight early the next morning and asked everyone else to stay in California and pray.

Keith drove me to LAX the next morning, and I arrived in Detroit that afternoon. Michael, Daddy's fraternity brother and friend, along with his wife, Donna, who had been friends with Mama, picked me up from the airport. Michael had stayed with Daddy in the hospital room since he had been admitted. God truly brought some wonderful individuals to rally around us. On the way, we stopped by the house so I could retrieve Daddy's health-care directive, then we quickly headed to the hospital.

As I walked into the hospital, I realized that it was the same hospital and the same wing where Mama had passed away. The nurse and doctors introduced themselves and shared Daddy's vitals. I made them aware that Daddy did not want to be a "vegetable" and that his healthcare directive clearly indicated he should not be kept on life support if that became the case. I asked them what tests needed to be run to assess his chances of regaining his ability to communicate and his mobility. The doctors very patiently said that a test to determine the amount of blood flowing through his brain would help, so they scheduled the test to be run the next day.

A childhood friend of Troy's and mine, Todd, picked me up from the hospital that first evening, took me to pick up some food, and dropped me off at the house. That night, I kneeled and prayed through tears for God to fully restore Daddy's health and told Him I could not lose both parents and my only sibling so close together. It was truly very strange and lonely being in my childhood home alone, knowing Mama and Troy were both gone and that Daddy was in the hospital fighting for his life.

I drove Mama's car to the hospital the next day and stayed with Daddy. I played music for him, spoke to him, and tried everything to get him to regain consciousness, but he did not. Later, when the nurse came into the room, I told her my mama had also been in the ICU in that hospital back in January. I told her about the two nurses, Jessica and Kate, and asked if they were still with the hospital. She told me they were and could facilitate introductions during their respective shifts. In the meantime, Daddy was retrieved so the all-important test could be run. Daddy's nurse returned with a pretty nurse about my height who introduced herself as Kate. Once I introduced myself and helped her remember Mama, she began crying. She told me she could not believe I was at the hospital experiencing a serious health scare with my dad after losing my mother and brother. She was so distraught, I actually had to console her. Kate was even more warm in person than she sounded over the phone. What a wonderful person Mama had with her, holding her hand while she passed. I thanked Kate for all she did for Mama and our family back in January.

Daddy was brought back to the room and one of the doctors wanted to speak with me. She said in a very kind voice that Daddy had no blood flowing through his brain. I asked her to clarify if this meant that he would, without a doubt, remain in his current state forever. She calmly said "Yes." I thanked her for the information and immediately called Keith and asked him to update the family while I contacted a few of his closest fraternity brothers to update them. One of my closest friends, Fraun, came to the hospital to sit with me and brought me food, as well. Daddy's hospital room was a revolving door of visitors, which I appreciated.

Later that evening, Fraun came by the house to visit for a while. It felt so good to have someone who not only knew me, but also knew Mama, Daddy, and Troy so well to just sit with me. Fraun had also attended the memorial service for Mama and Troy back in April and she was the Matron of Honor in my wedding. One of Daddy's fraternity brothers, Desmon Daniel, who is a pastor, also came by the house to sit with me and pray for my family. I felt so much better after these visits. It was very easy for me to make the difficult decision I knew I had to make.

Saying Goodbye to Daddy

I returned to the hospital the next day. I was alone and spoke to Daddy to let him know I was being brave and honoring his wishes to not remain a "vegetable." I told him that many individuals wanted to speak to him that day, then by the evening, he would be removed from life support and would be with the Lord.

I found the doctor and told him that I would like to allow Daddy's friends to visit him all day and at 6:00 p.m., after visiting hours, he could be removed from life support.

So many individuals wanted to visit Daddy. Due to COVID restrictions, only two could be in the room at a time, so they worked together to ensure this rule was followed. Some family members called my cell and asked me to hold the phone to Daddy's ear so they could talk to him and tell him how he had impacted their lives. The toughest phone call was from my daughter and son. They were sixteen and nineteen at the time. They took turns talking to Daddy, crying like I had not heard them cry since they were very young. They shared wonderful memories with him and told him how much he meant to them. They loved their grandparents and their Uncle Troy so much. The series of losses had been overwhelming for them. Keith did the same. Michael and Donna took me out to lunch to get me away from the hospital for a while, which I truly appreciated.

We returned a little later and it was getting close to the end of visiting hours. Pastor Karen and Gerald Cardwell, another pastor and well-respected and loved Kappa (who recently passed away due to COVID), came into the room to prepare for the transition. Daddy's nurse was also in the room. She rubbed my shoulders and comforted me the best she could. The two pastors read Scripture from their respective Bibles as Daddy was disconnected. I streamed the process so Keith, our children, and a few of our family members who were staying with them in Georgia could witness the transition. After Daddy passed, I packed up my things and walked out of his room. As I was walking down the hall, Daddy's nurse introduced me to Jessica, Mama's intake nurse. She was so pleased to meet me in-person but was also distraught about me losing so many family members so close together. She pointed to the room next to where we were standing and told me it was Mama's room. She also told me she loved my mama. I told her Mama loved her, too. We both cried and hugged each other.

The next day, Michael and Donna invited me over for a home-cooked meal. We laughed and shared stories about Daddy and Mama. I flew back home to Georgia two days later. Keith picked me up from the airport and I was so glad to be back home.

Later in July, we returned to Detroit for Daddy's wonderful memorial service. Most of our family from Nashville, Virginia, and North Carolina attended, along with a host of friends. At the beginning of the service, Kappa Alpha Psi Fraternity conducted their special burial service, which Daddy always enjoyed witnessing. Keith and I spoke, and multiple family members participated in the service. Keith thought it would truly add to the service to play the recording of the talk Daddy gave at Mama and Troy's service just a few months earlier. It was so moving, and it appeared that Daddy was eulogizing himself. The Kappas also sponsored the reception held after the service, which was quite delicious.

In October, we held a double interment service in Nashville so Daddy and Troy's ashes could be entombed with Mama's remains at the mausoleum. Daddy wanted to keep Troy's remains in Detroit with him until after he passed away. He said it gave him a sense of comfort. I promised Daddy I would have their ashes entombed with Mama's remains after he passed away, so the service brought me a sense of peace, knowing I was keeping a promise I made to Daddy.

Once again, the mausoleum was full of family and friends. Afterwards, some of my family members hosted a reception at our family home in Nashville. It felt so good being together. We are blessed to have each other.

Our family regrouped in November at our home for the Thanksgiving holiday. We had never hosted Thanksgiving for the family, but it felt like the right thing to do. We wanted to thank everyone for their support and spend time together without it being associated with a memorial or interment service. Michael and Donna along with their adult children travelled from Detroit to attend this very special three-day gathering. Another Kappa and good friend of Daddy's, Mike, who lives locally, attended, while Troy's friend Lowell and his wife Meredith also travelled from Indiana to celebrate with us. On Thanksgiving Day, we launched balloons in memory of Daddy, Mama, and Troy. It was a moving and memorable occasion.

The four of us spent Christmas at home and travelled to Hilton Head Island, one of our favorite destinations, for a few days during the New Year holidays. In a way, it felt good resuming some of our normal family traditions and getting away to the beach for a while. We looked forward to the approaching new year.

My Grief Journey: A Journal

Emotions, Truths, and Lies

My Grief Journey: A Journal

Emotions, Truths, and Lies

Overview

THE FOLLOWING SECTION summarizes the details of my grief journey by phase. These phases are personalized based on my own experience. Everyone's grief journey is different. I use the terms "emotions", "truths" and "lies" to describe my thoughts. You may find this helpful as well.

After reading the emotions and thoughts associated with my journey, review the questions that follow and journal your thoughts on the lined spaces provided.

Just as writing the details was very therapeutic for me, journaling the details of your personal grief journey, regardless of your current phase, will assist you with freeing your mind of sad and negative thoughts. In addition, writing down the positive feelings you are experiencing will allow you to reference these notes if those sad and negative thoughts return.

Each phase contains a scripture for reflection as you complete your journaling.

IMPORTANT:

Please keep in mind that while journaling is very therapeutic, sometimes it is necessary to seek additional help, especially if feelings of sadness, hopelessness and despair persist for many months, without subsiding. There are resources in the back of this book you may find helpful. In addition, it may be necessary to seek the help of a licensed mental health professional.

I. *The Dark Days* (January – April 2021)

My Emotions and Thoughts...

The months following the loss of Mama and Troy consisted of sadness, guilt, loneliness, disbelief, and a feeling of being separated from God. The Enemy was at work, filling my thoughts with lies, which made this an especially difficult time. My own personality characteristics of perfectionism and advocacy did not help the situation. I was also distracted a bit by overseeing the planning of the memorial service and developing the obituary programs leading up to the double memorial service scheduled in April 2021 for Mama and Troy.

I felt a great deal of guilt associated with the passing of Mama because Daddy and I made the decision to remove her from life support. I felt responsible for Mama's death and the part that ate me up was that I did not recall praying prior to making the decision.

I had this strange feeling that my loved ones, especially Mama, were still around somewhere, even though part of me knew this was not true. I also believed Mama was angry with me because she was not ready to go, even though I knew deep down inside, Mama would never feel that way. I kept thinking, Mama would never miss Christmas, so to just wait until Christmas. Mama would send tons of gifts as usual and frantically work to ensure all her beautiful decorations were placed in the home just right, prior to Christmas Eve.

I responded to all the texts and phone calls from friends and extended family, but I was honestly just going through the motions because I knew that isolating myself would not be a wise decision.

I could not understand how I was still able to function after the loss of two immediate family members. I thought I was either out of my mind or would be soon. There is no way I could be this strong–something was surely wrong.

I was also constantly on edge, waiting for the next loss to occur. I began to believe death was random and God was absent, just letting it occur. This was an attack on our family, and I had to be ready for the next devastating loss. After all, God did not answer my prayers for my loved ones to be healed, so He must not hear any of my prayers. I am on my own now.

Emotions

- ❖ Guilt associated with Mama's death
- ❖ Waiting for the next loss
- ❖ Alone and deserted by God
- ❖ Disbelief
- ❖ Sadness
- ❖ Believed my loved ones were still around

Lies

- ❖ I was responsible for Mama's death.
- ❖ God is not with me... He abandoned me.

❖ Death is random and God is absent.

❖ Since God did not answer my prayers for my family members to be healed, He does not hear any of my prayers.

The Dark Days

Think back to the first 3-4 months (or longer) after the loss(es) of your loved one(s).

How did you feel? Are some of the negative thoughts you were feeling at the time still with you? Were there some positive encounters you had with friends, acquaintances and family members that have helped you during the grieving process?

Please take time to document your thoughts and feelings below:

The Lord is close to the brokenhearted and saves those who are crushed in spirit. Psalm 34:18

Your Emotions and Thoughts...

II. *Daddy's Savior* (May – June 2021)

My Emotions and Thoughts...

After the memorial service, I expected to feel some sense of closure, but I did not. So instead, I focused on being Daddy's "savior" by ensuring he was happy every day. This, of course, was an impossible task, and it was partially driven by the guilt associated with my role in making the decision for Mama to be removed from life support. Since I was responsible for leaving Daddy alone in that house, it was my responsibility to see to it that he was not sad. Afterall, God had abandoned me, and I could no longer trust Him.

The daily calls to Daddy and spending Father's Day weekend with him were all driven by my desire to keep him happy. In the back of my mind, I knew this level of anxiety and constant worrying were unsustainable, but I could not stop, and I did not know how it could end. I sensed Daddy also knew this was not sustainable, but we never discussed it.

Emotions:

- ❖ Guilt associated with Mama's death
- ❖ Alone and deserted by God
- ❖ Sadness

❖ Anxiety associated with trying to keep Daddy happy

❖ Emotionally drained from long daily conversations with Daddy and daily worrying when I was not speaking with him

Lies:

❖ I was responsible for Mama's death.

❖ It was my responsibility to keep Daddy happy.

The Savior

Have you assumed the role of someone's savior?

This could be a parent, a child, or even a younger sibling. These feelings could be rooted in guilt, fear, the desire to feel in-control in the midst of chaos or to restore happiness in the life of a grieving loved one. This role is of course not sustainable, and it is very emotionally draining, but it is difficult to relinquish. Have you successfully relinquished this role or are you still grappling with these feelings? Do you need additional support to overcome these feelings? Does the person you are attempting to "save" need additional support?

Please take time to document your thoughts and feelings below:

Do not be anxious about anything, but in every situation, by prayer and petition, with thanksgiving, present your requests to God. And the peace of God, which transcends all understanding, will guard your hearts and your minds in Christ Jesus.
Philippians 4:6-7

Your Emotions and Thoughts...

_____

_____

_____

_____

_____

_____

_____

_____

_____

_____

_____

_____

_____

_____

III. *God Had a Different Plan*
(July – August 2021)

My Emotions and Thoughts...

Once during the time when I was feeling the most anxiety associated with believing I was solely responsible for Daddy's happiness, he and I had a conversation concerning his future. I told Daddy he could very well live for another twenty years or so. He told me, "God may have different plans."

Well, God certainly had different plans, considering Daddy's passing during July, less than six months after the passing of Mama and Troy. However, losing Daddy was also a turning point for me during my grief journey. Through the turmoil of facing my biggest fear at that time, I began to hear God again and feel His presence. At my lowest point is where I found Him.

I prayed repeatedly for God to heal Daddy while I was alone in my childhood home in Detroit. I got down on my knees and cried and begged God to save Daddy. I told Him I could not lose all three of my family members, but during those periods of prayer while sobbing and feeling I was at my lowest, I felt a warmth and a comfort I had not felt in a long time. I also came to realize while I was down on my knees that it was time for Daddy to go. I reflected on the wonderful one-on-one time I was blessed to have with him during the previous few months, even though some of those times were filled with anxiety and worry. I got to know even more fully how much Daddy loved me and he truly knew how much I loved him. Daddy also had a chance to review his succession plan with me in detail during Father's Day weekend. I knew it was time to let him go. The tears dried up and I fell asleep.

The next day at the hospital, when the doctor came into Daddy's room to share the results of the brain scan with me, I knew what she was going to say. Hearing that there was absolutely no blood flow through Daddy's brain validated even more that God was with me. I would not have to hear inconclusive test results and feel guilty again about removing a loved one from life support. God ensured the brain scan results were conclusive and Daddy ensured he provided me with a clear healthcare directive concerning his final wishes. Both gave me peace. My Father in heaven and my daddy on Earth worked together to provide me with that peace.

I began to view Daddy's passing as God's mercy. Daddy was in so much emotional distress after losing his entire household within eight days of each other, and I know he kept most of it bottled up inside. Even though Daddy and I knew our anxiety-filled daily conversations were not sustainable and did not know how they would end, God had a different plan. He accepted Daddy into His loving arms. He is at peace in heaven. I am at peace on Earth. We are both at peace.

Emotions:

- ❖ Fearful I would lose Daddy
- ❖ Sadness
- ❖ Comfort when I realized God was with me and has always been with me.
- ❖ Thankful that my Father in heaven and my daddy on Earth ensured I did not experience another episode of guilt associated with removing an immediate family member from life support based on inconclusive information.
- ❖ Peace in knowing Daddy is at peace in heaven with the Lord

The Truth:

- ❖ God has always been with me and never abandoned me.
- ❖ God loves me and I am His child.

Lies:

- ❖ I still bore some responsibility for Mama's passing.

Pivotal Moments

Are there events that have occurred during your grief journey which have positively impacted you in an unexpected way?

These could be brief encounters with strangers, impactful condolences expressed by friends or hitting the lowest point possible but rebounding in an uplifting manner.

Please take time to document your thoughts and feelings below:

Blessed are those who mourn, for they will be comforted. Matthew 5:4

Your Emotions and Thoughts...

IV. *Distractions* (*September – November 2021*)

My Emotions and Thoughts...

After Daddy's memorial service was held, I threw myself into executing his succession plan. Daddy was extremely organized and had everything in order. However, preparing the house in Detroit for sale and taking care of other loose ends kept me quite occupied.

After the double interment service for Daddy and Troy in October, we decided to host Thanksgiving for our extended family at our home in Georgia. Years ago, when our son was three, we began hosting a double birthday party (our children's birthdays are three days apart) at our home for all of our family, so this seemed very normal. This also allowed me to focus on preparing our home in Georgia for company and helping Keith, our primary cook, prepare a lavish meal. On Thanksgiving Day, we conducted a balloon launch in memory of Mama, Daddy, and Troy. We were all amazed that the balloons, stuffed with messages and packets of flower seeds, amazingly lifted effortlessly into the air, despite the added weight. We must have launched close to thirty balloons that day. It was so beautiful.

After Thanksgiving, the feelings of guilt returned. I decided it was time to seek additional help.

Emotions:

- ❖ Underlying guilt, despite the distractions
- ❖ Periodic sadness
- ❖ Busy and exhausted from focusing on executing Daddy's succession plan and preparing for the interment service and Thanksgiving

The Truth:

- ❖ God is with me.
- ❖ God never left me.

Lies:

- ❖ I still bore some responsibility for Mama's passing.

Distractions

Have you allowed distractions to prevent you from progressing with your grieving process?

After a loved one passes away, there are many tasks that must be completed, including planning services to honor our loved ones and reaching out to friends to thank them for their support. However, there are also activities that can be considered only distractions, including binging on TV shows, especially late into the night, significantly increasing the time spent on social media or surfing the web on your phone or computer. Some other very unhealthy distractions may include increasing your intake of alcohol or taking narcotics to numb the pain.

Additional support or professional help may be needed to overcome these distractions.

Please take time to document your thoughts and feelings below:

I will refresh the weary and satisfy the faint.
Jeremiah 31:25

Your Emotions and Thoughts...

V. Good-Bye Guilt
(December 2021 – January 2022)

My Emotions and Thoughts...

After the guilt began to resurface, once the distractions went away, I decided I needed some additional help. I reached out to my church, North Point Community Church[2], to learn more about their Restore[3] program that connects volunteer mentors with those experiencing grief. If I could find assistance anywhere, it would be North Point[2]. My childhood church, Calvin Presbyterian Church (now merged with Westminster Church of Detroit[1]) introduced me to Christ, but North Point[2] led me into a relationship with Christ. I completed an application online and within a couple of weeks, an individual by the name of Vickie reached out to me via email. She introduced herself and shared that she would be my grief mentor.

Vickie and I met for coffee. As soon as I met her, I felt comforted. She had such a warm, godly demeanor. After introductions, we shared our respective stories. I learned Vickie had also experienced a great deal of loss in her life. When it was my turn to speak, Vickie listened without saying a word. Once I was finished, she asked me about my goals during the meetings and I told her I was struggling with guilt associated with making the decision to have my mother removed from life support, which resulted in her passing.

Vickie looked at me and said, "You are not responsible for your mother's death. It was her time to go. God numbers our days." This provided me with a great deal of relief. It was something I felt deep down inside, but hearing someone else say it aloud validated my feelings. Vickie and I finished our conversation, scheduled our next weekly meeting, and warmly said goodbye. As I walked to my car, my steps seemed lighter, and I knew that only good would come out of these meetings with Vickie. I could not wait to get home to tell Keith about our discussion. Keith was so happy for me. He had expressed his concern about my emotional health due to the trauma of losing three immediate family members so close together. He believed I was holding everything inside and would one day crack.

A couple of days later, Vickie sent me an email containing a link to a video titled "A Godly Perspective on End-of-Life Decisions (Part 1 of 2)"[4] from a well-known ministry named Focus on the Family[5]. It was a talk given by an experienced trauma surgeon who helped families navigate end-of-life decisions according to Biblical principles. In the video, Dr. Kathryn Butler, a former trauma surgeon, shared a list of considerations a person should contemplate if they are faced with deciding whether a loved one should be removed from life support. The interesting part was that it had just aired on October 26, 2021, just one week before Vickie and I first met. It came just in time! Part of me was anxious to view it, hoping it would put to rest the guilt that kept resurfacing, but another part of me was scared to view it in case it reinforced my feelings of guilt. I waited a few days to view it and made sure I was relaxed and calm.

As I listened to this very kind and calming woman share this important information, I could not believe what I was hearing. As previously mentioned, part of the guilt I felt was associated with the fact that I did not recall praying after the doctor discussed the option of removing Mama from life support. I remembered calling Daddy, but I do not remember praying. I assumed Daddy suggested it and I coldly agreed to make a critical end-of-life decision. However, as I heard the list of considerations, I quickly realized I had contemplated all of them while listening to Mama's doctor and while speaking with Daddy over the phone. I did not coldly make a decision; I was listening to the Holy Spirit as it guided my thoughts and communicated with my spirit. I may have been too exhausted and shaken to pray, but the Holy Spirit was communicating with my spirit the entire time. I just did not remember.

I began to cry as I came to this realization, then I prayed, "Thank you, Lord, for Vickie. Thank you for this timely and loving video and thank you for communicating with my spirit when I was too exhausted and shaken to physically pray to You." A compelling statement the doctor said brought me considerable relief. "God does not need a ventilator to perform a miracle."[4] This gave me peace of mind knowing our days truly are numbered (as Vickie shared) and that God will only allow an individual to pass away if it is their time to go, with or without a ventilator or medications.

The next week, I could not wait to share my news with Vickie. During our meeting she was so pleased to hear the video provided me with some sense of peace and closure. Vickie and I finished our sessions by January 2022, but we continue to stay in touch via text and often bump into each other at church. God provided me with the perfect grief mentor who provided me with resources that were released at just the right time to uplift me and positively change the trajectory of my grief journey. Things do not just randomly occur so perfectly. God was truly at work.

Emotions

- ❖ Peace and comfort due to the wonderful Restore[3] curriculum and Vickie
- ❖ Comfort in knowing the Holy Spirit was communicating with my spirit when I was making the end-of-life decision about Mama, even when I could not pray

The Truth

- ❖ God allowed me to cross paths with individuals to serve as His hands and feet and lift the burden of guilt, permanently.
- ❖ God was with me when I was making end-of-life decisions regarding Mama.

No More Lies!

Negative Thoughts

Are there negative thoughts you cannot relinquish that continue to plague you?

These may be associated with fear, guilt, anger, or even worthlessness. It is important to journal these thoughts, but also discuss them with a trusted friend, family member, your local church or a licensed mental health professional.

Do you need additional support to work through these feelings so you can live the life God intended for you to live?

Please take time to document your thoughts and feelings below:

My flesh and my heart may fail, but God is the strength of my heart and my portion forever.
Psalm 73:26

Your Emotions and Thoughts...

VI. *The Winding Road of Grief*
(February – May 2022)

My Emotions and Thoughts...

After my sessions with Vickie ended, the guilt associated with Mama's passing never resurfaced. My childhood home was sold and I had addressed almost all of the loose ends associated with Daddy's succession plan. I felt I was truly on my way toward full acceptance of the passing of my loved ones; however, reaching full acceptance would not be a straight road.

Even though I understood as a Christian that my loved ones were with the Lord, I began to have second thoughts and became obsessed with thoroughly understanding the transition of the soul from death to heaven and how the second coming of Christ would impact this journey. When would I be reunited with my loved ones? Would we truly know each other? How would things change during the second coming of Christ? These questions continued to fill my head and I searched for the truth in the Bible and other publications, but nothing seemed to address them all clearly.

On the Friday before Mother's Day, my questions became more pressing. Our daughter, Brooke was out with friends, so Keith and I decided to go out to eat and walk around a local outdoor mall near our home. While eating, one of the pastors from our church, Bryan, noticed us and came over to say hello. We had not seen him for a few years. We also had not returned to church since it reopened after closing during the pandemic in 2020. Bryan always held a special place in our hearts because he had experienced a great deal of loss, as well, many of which were close together. He was the pastor who we met with for guidance periodically when Keith and I were married couple small group leaders at our church several years prior. Bryan is also one of the warmest and most gracious people we know.

We greeted him and took turns updating each other regarding our lives. I mentioned to Bryan the losses we recently experienced and he was so sorry to hear about them. We finished talking and wished Bryan well. After he left, I had an overwhelming feeling that I needed to attend church on Sunday. This seemed very strange, especially since Sunday was Mother's Day and I had no desire to set foot in church on Mother's Day and see all the attendees with their mothers. I told Keith about these feelings, and he graciously listened to me. On Saturday, I thought these feelings would subside, but they did not. Rather, they grew stronger. I knew I had no choice but to attend church the next day.

Keith, Brooke, and I attended church on Mother's Day (Austin was still away at college). I was having some second thoughts as we sat down, but part of me felt so much better returning to church. As usual, the worship time was so moving, and my second thoughts quickly melted away. As only God can do, as He had been showing me repeatedly during my grief journey, He heard me and He was with me. Of all the sermons that could have been given on Mother's Day, this sermon was titled "Heaven."[6] The pastor was at the end of a series that answered in detail all the questions that had been burdening me so much during the past few months. I could not believe it! I thanked God for always being with me, for hearing me, and I apologized for doubting Him. We have attended church every Sunday since that time. Brooke also decided to begin serving weekly in the pre-school environment. She began in this environment at age two when we first started attending North Point[2], so this is extra special to us.

Emotions

- ❖ Anxiety associated with my open questions concerning heaven and the transition of my loved ones' souls
- ❖ Gratitude to God for hearing me, loving me, and answering the questions that had been burdening me for so long

The Truth

- ❖ God is with me and loves me enough to answer all my questions.
- ❖ God has always been with me.

New Negative Thoughts

**Just when you thought you were through the
toughest part of the grieving process and all
your negative thoughts were eliminated, did new
ones arise?**

Just like your initial negative thoughts, it is important to journal
these thoughts, but also discuss them with a trusted friend, family
member, your local church or a licensed mental health professional.

**Please take time to document your thoughts and
feelings below:**

I can do all this through him who gives me strength.
Philippians 4:13

Your Emotions and Thoughts...

_____

_____

_____

_____

_____

_____

_____

_____

_____

_____

_____

_____

_____

_____

VII. *My Eternal Journey*
(June 2022–to Present)

My Emotions and Thoughts...

I still sometimes experience sadness due to the loss of my family members, but most of my days are happy ones. On some days, looking at old photographs of my loved ones brings me joy, but on other days I might feel sad. The same is true when I hear songs they once sang and loved. I know this is normal and I realize it will take time to overcome such a traumatic loss, but God is with me and has never let me down. I know He has important things that He wants me to do, and I also know the loss of my loved ones has made me more empathetic toward the plight of others.

The losses I have experienced are just part of my story here on Earth, and as hard and heartbreaking as those losses have been, they have made me a better person and are an integral part of my story, not just an interruption to it. I truly know this time on Earth is just a small segment of my eternal life. One day, I will come face-to-face with the Lord, and I will see and spend time with my loved ones forever. There will be no more COVID and no more brain hemorrhages to take them away from me.

I clearly understand that my acceptance of Christ as my Lord and Savior is all I need to enter heaven, and I understand Christ died for my sins and paid my ransom to provide me with this gift. Understanding this love and the hardships and pain experienced by the Lord on my behalf means I have absolutely no reason to spend my remaining days on Earth sad and moping around. Out of gratitude, I plan to spend my remaining days being the "hands and feet" of Christ to honor the memory of my loved ones, who lived their lives being the "hands and feet" of Christ.

Emotions:

❖ Both sadness and happiness as I view photographs of my loved ones and hear music they once loved

The Truth:

❖ God hears all my prayers and sometimes the answer is "no," but it does not mean He loves me any less.

❖ My loved ones are safe with the Lord, and I will see them again and we will know each other.

❖ The Lord wants me to be someone else's "good" while I am here on Earth.

Acceptance

Acceptance of the loss(es) of your loved one(s) does not mean you will never cry over their loss again and that you will not experience sad moments.

Are most of your days good ones? Have you resumed many of the activities you enjoyed prior to the loss(es) and maybe even started new ones? Do you enjoy social interaction with family and friends? Do you feel uplifted when you recall memories of your loved one(s)?

If you agree with most of the questions above, you have most likely accepted the passing of your loved one(s). If not, there may still be some work to do in the prior phases referenced. If needed, take some time to re-visit each of them and determine which feelings and/or negative thoughts are holding you back from accepting the loss(es) of your loved one(s). Also, determine if you need additional help to overcome these feelings and negative thoughts.

Please take time to document your thoughts and feelings below:

He will wipe away every tear from their eyes. …
There will be no more death, or mourning or crying
or pain, for the old order of things has passed away.
Revelation 21:4

Your Emotions and Thoughts...

_____

_____

_____

_____

_____

_____

_____

_____

_____

_____

_____

_____

_____

What I Know Now

What I Know Now

Understanding "Why"

I may never know the real reason why the Lord allowed my three loved ones to pass away so close together, but I do know:

- His timing is always perfect.
- God is in control and will always be in control.
- God is stronger than my circumstances.
- God answered Daddy's prayers regarding the order of the losses.
- Having a loving family as a child prepared me to weather the storm of 2021.
- I am a more empathetic person now than I was then.
- My family and I now do not take this time on Earth for granted.

- The losses of my loved ones and how I have responded have had a positive impact on many individuals.

What I Have Learned

- When you first lose a loved one, just cry, pray and accept help from others...this may be all you can do.
- Be patient with friends who may make insensitive comments; they are probably uncomfortable and are not sure of what to say.
- Pray and read the Bible, even when it feels like you are just "going through the motions"; one day, the words will begin to have an impact on you and will come alive.
- Telling your story of loss and the pain you feel over and over again helps. Find friends or family members who are willing to listen; the "heaviness" you feel will slowly lift. This will take time.
- As Christians, if we grieve in a healthy manner, trusting the Lord and depending on Him, when we lose someone we love, we grow even closer to the Lord and become more empathetic toward the plight of others.
- The loss of loved ones on a typical timeline has the potential to positively alter your character incrementally.
- The loss of loved ones on an accelerated timeline (like my experience) has the potential to positively alter your character exponentially.

- Along this eternal continuum timeline on which Christians are privileged to journey, if we are blessed to live a long life on Earth, we will experience heartache at some point. The questions are:
  - How will we respond?
  - How will we allow it to shape our legacy?
  - Will we allow it to end our story, or transform our story into something more beautiful?

"When something bad happens you have three choices. You can either let it define you, let it destroy you, or you can let it strengthen you."

— **Dr. Seuss**

Acknowledgments

I FIRST MUST THANK God for pushing me to write this book, and in record time! Before retiring at the end of 2020, after close to thirty-six years with an Atlanta-based Fortune 500 company, I knew I wanted to write during my retirement years, but I could not choose a topic. After losing three of my immediate family members within less than six months of each other in 2021, with two of those losses occurring in January, a month after I retired, I put that dream aside. Focusing on comforting my daddy during the short amount of time he lived after losing Mama and Troy, planning memorial and interment services, and executing Daddy's well-organized succession plan took all my time, energy, and mental capacity. After a year, I continued to deal with a lot of emotions and, once again, decided to put the dream of writing books aside.

The beginning of 2023 seemed like the right time to pursue my dream. After much prayer and quiet contemplation, I decided

I would write a book and journal about my grief journey, along with how God brought me through it and transformed me into a new person. I gave myself six to eight months to write the book, but God had a different plan. I tossed and turned each night until it was completed. Each day, I would sit and write at my computer for over four hours without taking any breaks. By the evening, I felt physically and emotionally drained. I would rest my mind for a day or so, then resume writing at the same pace. By the time I was done, the sadness and negative thoughts had been replaced with funny memories, gratitude, and joy. The experience was truly cleansing and therapeutic. I set out to write this book to help others who are grieving after a traumatic loss, but I now also believe God inspired me to write this book to help me fully accept the losses of my loved ones. The miraculous part is that it did not take me many months to write, as I originally estimated... It took me only four weeks to complete the full draft!

I also must thank my devoted husband of nearly thirty years and best friend, Keith. We have endured many good times and tough times, but through it all, we have always loved and supported each other. He loved Daddy, Mama, and Troy so much and drove me up and down the highway between Georgia and Detroit or Georgia and Nashville multiple times with no questions asked to be with Daddy, attend memorial and interment services, and prepare my childhood home for an estate sale as well as its ultimate sale.

I must thank my son and daughter, Austin and Brooke. God blessed us with two of the most loving, kind, hardworking, and supportive children, now young adults anyone could ever have. Despite

Austin's grueling academic schedule while studying architecture at a SEC college, he always cleared his agenda to be by our side when needed in 2021. As previously mentioned, he is responsible for the beautiful illustrations contained in this book. He also gave me some great feedback regarding my manuscript, which I incorporated.

Since COVID was still a huge health concern in 2021, Brooke attended high school remotely. She never once complained about having to complete the second half of her sophomore year in her Uncle Troy's room in Detroit at times, nor did she complain about all the trips she had to take with us in 2021. Austin and Brooke, know that your grandparents and your Uncle Troy loved you so very much. Their friends have shared many stories of their constant bragging regarding the two of you.

I want to thank Pastor Lee Jenkins, Senior Pastor of Eagles Nest Church[7] in Roswell, GA for taking the time to review my manuscript and write such a moving and thoughtful foreword for my book. Your time and effort are appreciated more than you know.

I am so thankful for my many aunts, uncles, and cousins who called me, sent text messages, travelled to Detroit and Georgia, invited us to a special Mother's Day dinner and a birthday celebration, hosted a reception after Daddy and Troy's interment service, and joined us in Georgia for Thanksgiving and a balloon launch during 2021, despite the pandemic. They are still supporting us today. I do not know how individuals who do not have such a loving and devoted extended family ever get through trials such as 2021. You mean more to me than I could ever express. I truly understand you are grieving, as well, but you have never let that stop you from always being there for me, and I appreciate all you have done and are still doing.

I need to thank my cousin, Janet, who encouraged me to write this book. She also lent her professional editing skills to help proof the book during its early stages. Her encouraging words and positive feedback regarding the book meant so much.

Throughout 2021, so many of my parents' and Troy's friends contacted me to provide comfort and to share stories or more. Some I knew previously, and some are new friends. Either way, their calls and text messages brought me comfort. I hope I brought them comfort, as well. Others were with me at the hospital before Daddy died, attended memorial/interment services, and others travelled to Georgia to spend Thanksgiving with us. Some of these friends include Ruth Betty, Pat and Merlton Brandenberg, Tammy Brandenberg, Donna and Michael Craighead, Chris Garrett, Phyllis and Carter Gilmer, Fraun Gray, Jalilah Haqq, Lowell and Meredith Harper, Todd Herron, Sperry Jones, Dr. Althea Masterson, Carrie Shipp, Bob Stokes and Mary and Charles Tisdale.

I want to thank other friends who were there for me, listened to my story, sent or delivered food to our home, or shared sympathetic words, including Tandreia Bellamy, Nette Blair, Barbara and Archie Bransford, Beth Brown, Kim and Dr. Marcus Brown, Joy Burns, Lisa and David Burns, Connie Cheren, Rhonda Clark, Stephanie and Robert Dobbs, Lisa and Van Emberger, Laura Cegala and Mark Goodman, Shawnda and Troy Henry, Gina Hutchins, Valerie Le, Donna Liberatore, Weyta and Mike Malone, Kelly and Rick Mosley, Christine Thio, and Loretta Willis.

I want to thank the men of Kappa Alpha Psi Fraternity Incorporated for their steadfast support and love expressed to our entire family, including hosting an over hour long Zoom call to comfort Daddy and lift him up with encouraging words shortly after Mama and Troy passed away, arriving at the church early on the day of Mama and Troy's memorial service to greet our family on a cold morning, visiting Daddy in the hospital and comforting me while I waited for test results, helping us sort through items in my childhood home after Daddy passed away, conducting the ceremonial burial service during Daddy's memorial service, sponsoring the reception after Daddy's memorial service, and so much more.

In addition to thanking the entire Kappa Alpha Psi organization, I would like to also thank the Kappas who supported our family on a more personal basis, including Grand Polemarch Reuben A. Shelton III who took the time to deliver a very kind and sincere acknowledgement of Daddy's many contributions via video during his memorial service, Andrew Fox, Jr., Southfield Chapter Polemarch, and the Kappa Men of the Southfield Chapter who assisted me with planning Daddy's memorial service, flooded the church with their presence during both memorial services, and assisted in so many ways. Desmon Daniel, who prayed with me and provided emotional support the evening I had to make the decision to have Daddy removed from life support. Gerald Cardwell, who recently passed away, but was at my side during Daddy's transition. Glenn Jackson, who brought breakfast to Daddy every Wednesday morning, in spite of his protests after Mama and Troy passed away, including the day he was rushed to the hospital. Dr. William Sharp, who was Daddy's physician and helped answer questions for me while Daddy was in the hospital. Ken Glass who sent photos and text messages to check in on me. Mike Washington who remains a good friend today and lives very close to us in Georgia. And last but not least, W. Michael Craighead and his wife, Donna, who have not left my side and have stepped in as an honorary aunt and uncle.

I want to thank all our friends from my childhood church (Calvin Presbyterian) who are now members of Westminster Church of Detroit[1], along with Pastor Karen and the staff members who worked so diligently to ensure the memorial services for Daddy, Mama, and Troy were extra special. Thank you in particular to Dorothy Cole and Dawn Hicks for lending their care and love toward planning the services, particularly the beautiful receptions after both services. Thank you to Gail and Robert Young as well as their daughter, Lisa Corneliussen, who travelled from North Carolina to attend both memorial services.

I want to thank my current church, North Point Community Church[2], for playing such a pivotal role in my ability to accept the losses of my loved ones. The curriculum provided by the Restore[3] program, along with support from my patient and caring Restore[3] mentor, Vickie, ultimately led to my ability to release the guilt I felt in conjunction with Mama's death. Vickie also provided me with a great deal of helpful feedback regarding my manuscript. Thank you to Bryan Apinis for inspiring us to return to church without even saying a word about it. Thank you to Suzy Gray for her support in coordinating the review of the North Point[2] and Restore[3] excerpts of the book.

I want to thank Focus on the Family[4] for providing exceptional resources. You played a key role in my healing.

Finally, thank you Mama, Daddy, and Troy for your consistent love and support, for the many stories you shared, for the songs you sang, for the laughter, for the encouragement, and for always being my cheerleaders. I will love you always.

Resources

1. Westminster Church of Detroit https://wcodetroit.org

2. North Point Community Church https://northpoint.org/

3. North Point Community Church – Restore Program https://northpoint.org/restore

4. Dr. Kathryn Butler, "A Godly Perspective on End-of-Life Decisions (Part 1 of 2)," Focus on the Family, October 26, 2021, https://www.focusonthefamily.com/episodes/broadcast/a-godly-perspective-on-end-of-life-decisions-part-1-of-2/.

5. Focus on the Family https://www.focusonthefamily.com

6. Pastor Joel Thomas, "Heaven (Part 3)–The Age to Come", North Point Community Church, May 8, 2022, https://northpoint.org/messages/heaven/the-age-to-come

7. Eagles Nest Church, Roswell, GA https://eaglesnestchurch.org/

8. Additional Resources: https://kjoynerbooks.com/resources/

Printed in the USA
CPSIA information can be obtained
at www.ICGtesting.com
JSHW041638050823
46008JS00005B/29